# Intr‹

Something wonderful has happened. It occurred in the middle of the 1800's and it caught the attention of the world. It grew quickly in popularity, so fast that many in positions of power went on a crusade to stamp it out.

Why? Because it provided answers to questions that we all have been searching for. Questions that have been posed by philosophers since the beginning of time were asked and the results fully described.

Why such fear by the ruling religious classes? Because it explained the purpose for our life without dogma, without having to ask a priest or reverend for forgiveness. No special clothes to wear, no diet restrictions. No requirement for a specialized building or monthly stipends.

Why was it scorned? Because it didn't use the word "sin". It talked of spirits. It told us we could come back as either sex. And when it was asked about marriage, we were told that marriage is between two spirits, not two sexes.

We were told that a marriage should be the union of two spirits for as long as they work together in harmony. If not, then it wasn't the spirit world that stopped people from parting, it was our erroneous human convictions.

The organized Christian religions reacted strongly. They burned books and harassed those that knew and cherished the fact that the Third Revelation had occurred.

Like other messages of love, charity and fraternity before; this one was met with strong opposition. Ideas are hard to stamp out and this one is growing again. The world is re-awakening to Spiritism.

Learn what Spiritism is and how it can positively shape your life and happiness.

*Spiritism 101 – The Third Revelation*

# Spiritism 101

The Third Revelation

By

Brian Foster

—————◆—————

http://www.nwspiritism.com/

1st Edition

# Table of Contents

# Chapter 1 – The Promise of Spiritism

I want to give you good news. You are immortal. Your spirit will live forever. You will experience life after life in a quest to perfect yourself. You have a mission, the most important mission possible; to improve, to love, to be charitable. To be part of a grand plan to not only raise yourself, but your neighbors and the entire human race to where the earth will truly be a paradise.

We are destined to live on a planet where hatred, discord and wars are a thing of the past. Where envy and malicious gossip is an aberration. Where we spend the majority of our waking hours in harmonious work to help others, not to gain advantage over co-workers or climb as quickly as possible to the top.

How do we know all of this? Because, of the gift of knowledge from God and Jesus. The first revelation was from Moses, who set the stage for the concept of one God. The second was from Jesus, who brought the concept of eternal love and forgiveness to us. In the 1850's the third revelation came. It was promised to us in the New Testament.

## Jesus Promised Us more Information

"If you love me, keep my commands. And I will ask the Father, and he will give you another Consoler to help you and be with you forever…the Spirit of Truth. The world cannot accept him, because it neither sees him nor knows him. But you know him, for he lives with you and will be in you." New Testament John 14: 15-17

"But the Consoler, the Holy Spirit, whom the Father will send in my name, will teach you all things and will remind you of everything I have said to you." New Testament John 14: 26

The prophecy was fulfilled. In the 1850's The Spirit of Truth began to communicate with us. Opening doors to the life beyond our existence and its meaning which few of us suspected.

We were told, that we, as immortal spirits come to earth to

improve. We are granted the opportunity to don a physical form in order to transform ourselves into loving, caring and honest individuals. That we are assigned to this school of earth for as many lifetimes as required to attain a pure state.

What did the Consoler actually say? What did The Spirit of Truth contribute? The Spirit of Truth through the work and efforts of Allan Kardec, who is known as the Codifier, presented the messages of the Spirit of Truth (Consoler) and that in the five books that Allan Kardec assembled, he revealed the extent of the Spirit world, who is God and Jesus, why we are here on earth, how we should live and the doctrine to follow. That is all. The answers to questions that every one of us have spent restless nights pondering.

Messages that aren't crouched in fire and brimstone. No mention of eternal hell or sins that can never be rectified. Instead we are presented with a tour de force of the vastness and the complex processes of the Divine Universe. We are succinctly told who is God, why we are here, why the world is simultaneously a beautiful and terrifying place and what are the guidelines to ascend to a better place.

## Allan Kardec

Let's start at the beginning with the person who facilitated the messages from The Spirit of Truth. Allan Kardec is the pen name of the French teacher and educator Hippolyte Léon Denizard Rivail (Lyon, October 3, 1804 – Paris, March 31, 1869).[1] Wikipedia describes his early life;

Rivail was born in Lyon in 1804. He was raised as a Catholic. He was a disciple and collaborator of Johann Heinrich Pestalozzi, and a teacher of mathematics, physics, chemistry, astronomy, physiology, comparative anatomy and French in Paris. For one of his research papers, he was inducted in 1831 into the Royal Academy of Arras. He organized and taught free courses for the underprivileged.[2]

Allan Kardec, was fifty-one years old when he first

encountered spirits. Anna Blackwell, who translated his books into English in 1881, describes his first encounters and what set him off in his journey;

"When, about 1850, the phenomenon of "table-turning" was exciting the attention of Europe and ushering in the other phenomena since known as "spiritist", he quickly divined the real nature of those phenomena, as evidence of the existence of an order of relationships hitherto suspected rather than known, namely, those which unite the visible and invisible worlds. Foreseeing the vast importance, to science and to religion, of such an extension of the field of human observation, he entered at once upon a careful investigation of the new phenomena. A friend of his had two daughters who had become what are now called "mediums." They were gay, lively, amiable girls, fond of society, dancing, and amusement, and habitually received, when "sitting" by themselves or with their young companions, "communications" in harmony with their worldly and somewhat frivolous disposition. But, to the surprise of all concerned, it was found that, whenever he was present, the messages transmitted through these young ladies were of a very grave and serious character; and on his inquiring of the invisible intelligences as to the cause of this change, he was told that "spirits of a much higher order than those who habitually communicated through the two young mediums came expressly for him, and would continue to do so, in order to enable him to fulfill an important religious mission."[3]

He was extremely interested in this message of a mission and wished to delve deeper. He discussed with his wife how he could ask and organize a series of questions to get a more complete understanding of the spirit world. His wife, Amelie, encouraged him to undertake this task. Given his background, he organized a series of questions that would be posed by mediums to spirits. Allan Kardec was not a medium himself, so he used the service of various mediums to gather the information. He did not rely on one reply, but made sure that an answer to one question was seconded by another medium in a different location.

Allan Kardec was careful to present Spiritism as the work of the spirits. Not a new religion dreamed up by one person, but a work of many incarnated mediums conversing with various spirits. The spirits were coordinated by The Spirit of Truth and the mediums were managed by Allan Kardec.

Allan Kardec wrote five books (*The Spirits' Book*, 1857; *The Mediums' Book*, 1861; *The Gospel according to Spiritism*, 1864; *Heaven and Hell*, 1865; *Genesis*, 1868), each dealing with separate subjects, but at the same time overlapping in their complete description of the Spiritist doctrine. The first and most famous is *The Spirits' Book*; he was given the title by his spirit messengers.

## What is Spiritism?

The basic tenets of Spiritism are:

1. Love God.

2. Do unto others as you would have others do unto you.

3. Practice justice.

4. Forgive all who offend you.

5. Make amends for our own wrong doing.

The spirits revealed to us the basic facts of our existence:

1. Your soul is immortal.

2. You travel through multiple lives as a process to learn to love, be fraternal, and be selfless.

3. The goal of God is for every spirit to one day be pure.

4. There is no eternal hell, it is a station for souls who are materialistic and have an excessive love of self.

5. There are many levels of heaven. Heaven is not a place where we have eternal leisure, but one of on-going work to help others.

6. Life on earth is like a school. You are assigned events in your life and how you react and behave will determine your spiritual progress.

In the 1930's in Brazil, the medium Chico Xavier began psychographing (the process of a medium writing under the direction of a spirit) messages and books sent by spirits. From the very beginning he was told to always follow the doctrines of Allan Kardec. Chico wrote more than 400 books by the time of his death in 2002. Within these books, the spirits revealed information about Allan Kardec and the spirit world's plan for our future;

1. When Jesus referred to the "Great Consoler", he was foretelling the arrival of the Spirit of Truth, which was codified by Allan Kardec.

2. For the earth to progress, the human race needs to understand that every action they do here on earth will have consequences in their next life.

3. The Bible was written by men under the influence of their beliefs and culture at their time. While the central spiritual message of love is eternal, the stories of the Bible, such as the Earth created in six days are allegories and not meant to be taken literally.

4. We are being told this now because the human race is culturally and technically advanced to be able to accept these messages.

5. Spiritism is not meant to replace religions, but to supplement them with the knowledge of the basic doctrine of reincarnation and its purpose.

6. The spreading and acceptance of Spiritism will enable to world to begin a new age, where war is a thing of the past.

7. The spirit world has planned these events and is guiding the earth through subtle interventions.

8. At some time in the future, science will definitely prove the existence of a soul and an afterlife.

All of the above is built on a foundation of love. With love God created the universe, with love God created spirits, with love God created man, so young spirits would have a method to comprehend that without love nothing good can be obtained.

These are the messages given to us by the spirit world via Allan Kardec and Francisco (Chico) C. Xavier. Others have echoed the same message. Authors who discuss the problems of life with spirits, by people who have had past life regressions and by those who had NDEs (Near Death Experiences). Gurus and religious leaders have sent us parts of the same communication, over and over. We just need to listen.

The spirit world is constantly connecting to mediums to alert us of a life beyond our single human existence. People from all cultures, all walks of life are reporting the same philosophy of love and redemption through trials.

None of these revelations are new. All have been told to us in one form or another for thousands of years. What is new, is the completeness, the opening of the curtain of mystery that surrounded the other side for so long. The spirit world desires us to rebalance our lives between materialism and spiritualism, to re-learn to selflessly care for others, for the goal of advancing ourselves and those around us to a new level.

# Chapter 2 – A Message from the Spirit of Truth

First let's explore the tone of the messages from the spirit realm. In Allan Kardec's book, *The Gospel According to Spiritism*, there is a communication from the Spirit of Truth, via a medium in Paris in 1860;

"I have come, as I once came amongst the wayward children of Israel, to bring the truth and dissipate the darkness. Listen to me. Spiritism, as my word of old, must remind disbelievers that above them reign the immutable truth; the good God, the great God who makes the plant germinate and raises the tides. I have revealed the divine Doctrine, and like a reaper, I have gathered into sheaves the good scattered amid humankind and have said, 'Come unto me, all you who suffer!'

However, ungrateful men and women have strayed from the straight and broad way that leads to the kingdom of my Father, and have become lost on the bitter path of impiety. My Father does not want to annihilate the human race; he wants you, through the help you give to one another – both the living and the dead, that is, dead according to the flesh, since death does not exist – to succor one another, and for the voice of the prophets and apostles no longer to be heard, but instead, the voice of those who have departed from the earth, proclaiming to you, 'Pray and believe! For death is resurrection and life is the chosen trial during which your cultivated virtues must grow and develop like cedar.'

O frail humans, who are aware of the darkness of your minds, do not stray from the beacon that divine clemency has placed in your hands to light your way and lead you, as lost children, back to the bosom of your Father.

I am too moved with compassion for your miseries, your great frailty, not to extend a sure hand to those wayward unfortunates who, seeing heaven, fall into the abysses of error.

Believe, love and meditate upon the things that are being revealed to you. Do not mix tares with the good seed, utopias with the truth.

O Spiritists! Love one another; this is the first teaching. Educate yourselves; this is the second. All truths are found in Christianity. The errors that have become rooted within it are of human origin; and here, beyond the grave – which you believed was nothingness – voices cry out to you: 'Brothers and sisters! Nothing perishes. Jesus Christ is the victor over evil; be victors over impiety.'[4]

What are the themes contained within this missive? First and foremost and try to love one another. No great apocalypse is planned to wipe us out. Only a plea to work together and support each other. Next, a request that we make an effort to learn what the spirit world requires of us.

The wonderful aspect of Spiritism, is the more you read, the more you are motivated to learn. The entire arc of our lives is exposed. Why did we have to endure the trials that were presented to us? Which seemed random at the time, but were in fact part of a plan. A plan to jog us out of complacency and into the right frame of mind to think beyond the next pleasure.

# Chapter 3 – The Triple Aspect of Spiritism

Spiritism does not ask you to possess blind faith. In fact it discourages it. According to Spiritism, miracles don't occur. All phenomena has an explanation.

Do we have absolute proof that God or spirits exist? As of yet no, but Spiritism tells us that one day it shall occur. For Spiritism is not meant to be a fossilized dogma but an ever expanding pool of knowledge.

Knowledge that will be brought to us by our scientists and by the spirit world. As we grow morally and technically, more will be presented to us.

Spiritism is a dynamic doctrine. It has three aspects that work together to provide the scaffolding which encompass the ever growing pool of knowledge.

First is philosophy. *The Spirits' Book* laid the foundation for the relationship between the spirit world and the physical world. The eternal questions of our creation, our creator, our destiny and our soul are all covered within Spiritism.

Second is science. This is the area which certainly would have the most doubters. Rightly so, for nothing has been proven to date. Modern society accepts people's belief in God, but only as a nod to those that need it.

What is not in question is the ground swell of studies about Near Death Experiences (NDE) and the retention of thought after all physical brain activity has ceased. The internet now allows people to compare their stories of premonition, talking with spirits and mediums who have knowledge about personal facts which would be improbable for them to know.

All of these, many of us are aware of and comfortable that there is a world beyond our senses. While others scoff as nonsense any unexplainable event, we mark it down to one more data point that promotes our feeling that our knowledge is limited and there are many things that are still unfathomable by science.

For now, Spiritism leans on the information provided by mediums throughout the world. Books, such as the ones psychographed by Chico Xavier, are continually being created, with the help of the spirit world. Books which little by little reveal more about the earth, our destiny and the complex workings of the spirit realm which looks over us.

Third is religion. To be clear, Spiritism does not consider itself to be a religion. Spiritism is a Doctrine. A way of life. There are no rites, no churches or temples, and no one who would function as a priest.

There is a moral code. A set of Divine Laws that is implanted into each us so we may instinctively sense the right path. Whereas, our desire for material goods often masks our good intentions, we do realize what we should or should not have done. And this is precisely the basis for our struggle on earth.

Once we are able to follow the road of love, charity, and selflessness we shall leave this period of our education and begin the next.

# Chapter 4 – Who and What is God

The first question in *The Spirits Book* is:

*Question 1. What is God?*

"God is the Supreme Intelligence – First Cause of all things."[5]

Allan Kardec lists six attributes about God:

1. God is *eternal*. If He had had a beginning, He must either have sprung from nothing, or have been created by some being anterior to Himself. It is thus that, step by step, we arrive at the idea of infinity and eternity.

2. God is *unchangeable*. If He were subject to change, the laws which rule the universe would have no stability.

3. God is *immaterial*, that is to say, that His nature differs from everything that we call matter, or otherwise, He would not be unchangeable, for He would be subject to the transformations of matter.

4. God is *unique*. If there were several Gods, there would be neither unity of plan nor unity of power in the ordaining of the universe.

5. God is *all-powerful* because He is unique. If He did not possess sovereign power, there would be something more powerful, or no less powerful, than Himself. He would not have created all things and those which He had not created would be the work of another God.

6. God is *sovereignty just and good*. The providential wisdom of the Divine Laws is revealed as clearly in the smallest things as in the greatest and this wisdom renders it impossible to doubt either His justice or His goodness.[6]

The Spiritist concept of God is not unlike others postulated by various religions. Given all of the above, we really still don't understand God. Only that the concept of what God truly is, is beyond us.

Allan Kardec asks the same question:

*Question 10. Can man comprehend the essential nature of God?*

"No; he lacks the sense required for comprehending it."[7]

Next, he poses the question that we all ask after trying, but failing to understand the nature of God:

*Question 11. Will man ever become able to comprehend the mystery of the Divinity?*

"When his mind shall no longer be obscured by matter, and when, by his perfection, he shall have brought himself nearer to God, he will see and comprehend Him."[8]

Sometime in the far future we shall be able to understand the Divine Being that is responsible for our creation. Until that day we should be thankful we live in a universe built on love.

# Chapter 5 – What is a Spirit?

We are spirits. The vast majority of our existence will be as a spirit. Our time in physical bodies are meant as periods of training or missions to help other spirits.

## How Spirits are Created

We know that as a physical body we are born of a mother. But how are we created as spirits? The Spirits Book supplies us with a non-answer:

*Question 81. Are spirits formed spontaneously, or do they proceed from one another?*

"God created them as he creates other creatures, by His will. But we must repeat again that their origin is a mystery."[9]

Therefore, we do not know exactly how we started. As you become a higher spirit you shall have the ability to remember more of your past lives and history, but I have never read or heard of any report coming from the spirit world concerning the first beginning of a spirit.

We are immortal, meaning that we shall watch the sun of our solar system turn into a red dwarf and eventually degrade into a lifeless body, with nothing but frozen rocks rotating around it.

Think about this for a moment. We worry what will happen tomorrow, or next week. Anxieties such as can we buy that new car, or will we be able to make the house payment. How do any of these concerns stack against the fact that no matter what happens, you can't die.

## The Spirit Form

You may lose your physical body, but the real you will never perish. So, what does the real you look like?

*Question 88. Have souls a determinate, circumscribed, and unvarying form?*

"Not for eyes such as yours; but, for us, they have a form though one only to be vaguely imagined by you as a flame a gleam, or an ethereal spark."[10]

We are energy with some matter thrown in. We can move at the speed of thought or take a leisurely walk. It all depends on our thoughts. In the spirit world, thought is action. Let me repeat again, thought is action.

This is one of the most important lessons that Spiritism supplies us. Here in our physical form, we learn that if we can just keep our mouth shut everything will be ok. Not true in the other world. Therefore, here on earth, in this chaotic location, we need to bear down and learn how to control our thoughts.

You can't just do good works and appear to like your fellow humans, you must feel love and fraternity from the bottom of your heart. For when you live in the spirit realm, your thoughts are an open book.

## Where Spirits Live

Where do you live the vast majority of your existence? The answer is everywhere. The entire universe will someday be yours to roam. The higher you ascend the larger your range.

*Question 87. Do spirits occupy a determinate and circumscribed region in space?*

"Spirits are everywhere; the infinitudes of space are peopled with them in infinite numbers. Unperceived by you, they are incessantly beside you, observing and acting upon you; for spirits are one of the powers of Nature, and you are the instruments employed by God for the accomplishment of His providential designs. But all spirits do not go everywhere; there are regions of which the entrance is interdicted to those who are less advanced."[11]

Unbeknownst to most of us, we swim in a sea of spirits. Good, bad and indifferent spirits, all able to detect our presence and know what we are thinking. This too is part of our training.

We must learn to not pick up other thoughts and let them affect our drive to perform what our conscience tells us is right. For there are many out there who love to see the daily disasters that we humans fall into every day.

Why can't we see them? Well, there are some people who actually can see spirits. They are mediums with an ability to view the spirit form. For the rest of us, we walk through the presence of spirits blind to their existence.

The spirit world exists on a different dimension. Scientists are correct, there are planes and dimensions surrounding us that we can't perceive. To the spirit world we are spirits locked in a case of dense matter. Our suit that protects us also severely restrains our senses.

## Levels of Spirits

You now are aware that we live in the midst of spirits. That there are many different types of spirits. Upfront, I want to let you know that when we die, we don't become intelligent caring angels of mercy. We become spirits which retain our memories, personalities and character we had during our physical life. In other words, people who were mean and petty in life are the same in death, people who were caring, kind and always willing to lend a helping hand in life are the same in death.

This is why we are here on this planet. God is not going to let uncaring, immature spirits loose on the universe. We must finish our assigned courses and graduate before we will be given the right to ascend.

Given the varieties of humans on the planet, it should be no surprise to learn about the different levels of spirits which reside amongst us.

The spirit realm tells us there are an unlimited number of levels of spirits, but for our consumption *The Spirits Book* has divided spirits into the following orders:

Third Order – Imperfect Spirits: Predominance of matter over spirit. These types of spirits are more influenced by material desires. They have a predilection for evil. They are ignorant, full of false pride and selfish. Within the third order, they are further divided into five class. All detail about these types of spirits are covered from question 100 to 106.

Second Order – Good Spirits: Predominance of spirit over matter. These spirits desire to ascend. They possess many qualities for good. Although they still have imperfections to repair. Good spirits are further divided into 4 classes. Questions 107 to 111 describe each class of good spirits.

First Order – Pure Spirits: These spirits are pure energy. They possess an intellectual and moral superiority over all others. Pure spirits no longer have to suffer through reincarnations. First order spirits are describe in question 113.

All of us one day will become pure spirits. We are in the middle of that process now. It all depends on our hard work and dedication for how fast we are able to attain perfection.

# Chapter 6 – The Spirit Realm

The spirit realm is the entire universe and not just the universe that we detect, but all of the universes. We are told the spirit universe was created first and our physical, denser universe was created after.

## The Beginning of the Universe

Allan Kardec in the book, *Genesis*, tells us what he learned from various spirits on how creation began:

"After having gone back – human limitations notwithstanding – to the hidden fount from which worlds derive like drops of water flowing from a river, let us consider the progress of the successive creations and their development.

The primitive cosmic matter contained the material, fluidic and vital elements for all the universes that unroll their magnificence before eternity. It is the fertile mother of all things, the first grandmother, and what is more, the eternal generatrix. This substance from which all the sidereal globes have come has not disappeared: this power is not dead, for it still gives birth incessantly to new creations, and receives incessantly the reconstituted elements of the worlds that have been effaced from the book of eternity."[12]

Our sun has a definite life, even our own universe, in which our galaxies rotate, has a life which at some distant future will run out of energy. Leaving only barren rock and a faint afterglow. This is what our science knows today.

What Spiritism teaches us is that our universe was born, probably from the matter left over from an extinguished universe, in a cycle that will flow forever. As immortal spirits we shall inhabit new universes.

The element that created the universe is called cosmic fluid. From this all else flows. It is everywhere and fills everything. In different combinations and densities, it is responsible for all planets, suns and life.

*Genesis* tells us more:

"This fluid penetrates bodies like an immense ocean. In it resides the vital principle that gives rise to the life of beings and perpetuates it on each globe according to its condition, a principle which in its latent state lies dormant as long as no voice calls upon it. By virtue of this universal vital principle, every creature, mineral, plant, animal, or other – because there are many other kingdoms of nature whose existence you do not even suspect – knows how to appropriate the conditions for its existence and lifespan."[13]

Nothing written in *Genesis* violates what we now know. String theory, multiple dimensions, even the statement that we do not know other kingdoms of nature, fit nicely into what we have been told by the spirit world. *Genesis* was written in the 1850's, the vast discoveries about viruses and other types of microbes still remained in the future at that time.

Later pages tells how when nebula form, the energies released from that rough sphere, veer off to create solar systems, suns, planets and moons. Again, while not divulging specific new scientific facts, the broad outline of our creation is consistent to what we understand today.

Which brings me to an important point. The spirit realm only reveals to us what we are able to comprehend. They don't send us radical theories. The spirit world will send advanced spirits to first plant the seeds, so at a later date we would be able to understand what they are presenting.

## The Planet Earth

Earth wasn't created in six days. It took billions of years. Spiritism doesn't force you to ignore the mass of data which makes the case for a slow evolution of our planet and life upon it.

There are differences from what we have learned. The first and by far is the major revelation that while evolution certainty causes

22

changes to life on earth over time, the process is guided and sometimes pushed along in a certain direction by the spirit world. Using the set of Divine Laws given to us by God, the spirit world is able to manipulate events and pathways to the creation of different forms of life.

In the book, *On the Way to the Light*, by Francisco C. Xavier, dictated to him by his spirit mentor Emmanuel, the originations of the earth and who guides us is revealed:

"The tradition of the spirit world say that, in the governance of all the phenomena of our system, there is a Community of Pure spirits, chosen by the Supreme Lord of the Universe, whose hands hold the guiding reins of the life of all planetary collectivities.

From what we have been told, this Community – made up of perfected, angelic beings, of which Jesus is one of the divine members – has met in the vicinity of the earth only twice in the course of the known millennia to decide urgent issues pertaining to the organization and direction of our planet.

The first meeting took place when the terrestrial orb detached from the solar nebula so that the demarcations of our cosmogonic system and the prototypes of life in the fiery matter of the planet could be set in space and time. The second occurred when the Lord's coming to the earth was determined in order to bring the immortal lesson of his Gospel of love and redemption to the human family."[14]

We are told that the earth was deliberately formed for the express purpose to use our planet as a place to incarnate spirits. The master of the entire operation, from setting our planet in orbit, the creation of the moon, manufacturing of the ozone layer to protect all organic forms, to the beginning of life until today is Jesus.

Chosen by God to be the Lord of earth. Jesus set forth the blueprints and utilized Divine Laws to construct an inhabitable oasis where humans could evolve and thrive.

# How Life Was Manufactured

The creation of life was not left to mere chance. There was a plan and it was followed. *On the Way to the Light* lets us in at the beginning:

> "Like modern engineering, which constructs a building foreseeing the tiniest requirements for it ultimate purpose, the artists from the spirit realm built the world of cells, initiating in primeval days the construction of the organized, intelligent forms of the centuries to come.
>
> Regarding the earliest cellular constructions, the ideal of beauty was their main concern from the start.
>
> That is why throughout time, beauty, combined with order, has been one of the indelible marks of all creation.
>
> Forms for all the kingdoms of nature were studied and foreseen. The fluids of life were manipulated so they could be adapted to the physical conditions of the planet; thus, the cellular constructions were fashioned according to the capabilities of the earth's environment. Everything, obeyed a plan pre-established by the merciful wisdom of the Christ in accordance with the laws of the beginning and of the overall development."[15]

Models from other planets were used to form the basis of flora and fauna of earth. Next, they were modified to thrive in our conditions. As life forms evolved, throughout the various periods, starting with the Precambrian, small modification were continuously made to direct the evolutionary paths of creatures on earth.

What we call natural laws, which are in fact Divine Laws, established when the universe was created, were used in ways we have not yet discovered to facilitate the entire arc of the earth's existence.

## What is the Spirit World Around the Earth

The spirit realm is throughout the universe, but for us, we are mainly concerned about our immediate surroundings.

Roughly, the sphere of influence of the earth can be broken down into three areas.

First, at the highest level is what is considered heaven. Where good spirits ascend. Second, is the Lower Zone, where we, the incarnates, live. We live side by side with spirits who also reside in the Lower Zone. Thirdly, is the Abyss, or as we call it; Purgatory (not really Hell, since no one is condemned forever).

## The Abyss

Let's start from the bottom and work our way up, since that is how most spirits have travelled through their multiple lives.

The Abyss: It is where the opposite of the Golden Rule reigns, others do unto you as you have done unto others. The spirit realm doesn't call it "Hell", for that would imply a location where errant souls go and stay permanently. The spirit realm calls it the Darkness or the Abyss, sometimes I see it mentioned as a type of purgatory.

For spirits never are sent to unalterable situations. God wishes all of us to eventually ascend to be a pure spirit. Even though the journey may be torturous and painful. Whenever we find ourselves in real spiritual pain, it is usually because a nice suggestion wasn't absorbed, hence we required a blunter object to attract our attention. The Darkness is a weighty sharp weapon which is specifically designed for those of us who just wouldn't take the hint.

The Darkness starts at the crust of the earth and flows downward. Andre Luiz, in the book *Liberation*, travels on a mission to the Abyss, he describes the landscape;

"The sun's light looked different.

A grayish haze clouded the entire sky.

Volitation (*definition: ability to move by thought*) was impossible.

The vegetation looked sinister and afflicted. The trees were almost bare and the nearly-dry branches looked like arms lifted in supplication.

Large, foreboding birds that looked sort of like ravens were cawing like little winged monsters eyeing hidden prey.

What was most troubling, however, was not the bleak landscape – it was somewhat similar to others I had experienced – but the piercing appeals coming from the mire. Humanlike groans came in every tone."[16]

The scenes described could be out of any of the movies or books we have seen and read about hell. A desolate landscape, dry and populated with revolting creatures.

Andre also notices gangs, which are wandering around the landscape:

"From time to time, hostile groups of deranged spirit entities passed in front of us, indifferent and incapable of noticing our presence. They were speaking loudly in broken but intelligible Portuguese, their laughter betraying deplorable conditions of ignorance. They were dressed in sinister attire and carried implements for fighting and wounding."[17]

What is the purpose of the Darkness? The question is answered in the book, *Between Heaven and Earth*, by Francisco C. Xavier, dictated by the spirit Andre Luiz.

Andre asks his team leader why are there areas of purgatory? Andre receives the following answer:

"The sickly bird does not stop being sick just because it escapes from its cage. Hell is a creation of imbalanced souls who have come together in one place, just as the miry bog is a collection of slimy nuclei that congregate together. When, with a consciousness inclined toward good or toward evil, we perpetrate this or that crime, we really can wound and harm someone, but more than that, we are wounding or harming ourselves. If we kill our neighbor, our victim will receive so much sympathy from others that he or she will soon be reestablished within the laws of equilibrium that govern us, and will often come to our aid before we can recompose the dilacerated threads of our conscience. When we harm this or that person, we actually harm our own soul first, because we lower our dignity as eternal spirits, delaying our sacred opportunities for growth."[18]

There are many levels of the Darkness, none of them pleasant. Only those who are compelled to live with souls similar to themselves are sent there. And a spirit lingers only until the time he or she comprehends, from the bottom of their soul that love, not hatred, envy, revenge or any form of domination is the true path.

### The Lower Zone

What exactly is the Lower Zone like? Andre Luiz, who woke up there after his death on the operating room table describes one small part of it:

"Actually, I felt like a prisoner trapped behind dark bars of horror. With my hair on end, my heart pounding, and scared stiff, I often cried out like a madman. I begged for mercy and clamored against the painful despondency that had taken hold of my spirit. But when the loud cries didn't fall on an implacable silence, they were answered by lamenting voices even more pitiful than my own. At other times, sinister laughter rent the prevailing silence. I thought that some unknown companion out there was a prisoner of insanity. Diabolical forms, ghastly faces, animal-like countenances appeared from time to time, increasing my panic."[19]

Doesn't seem like a great place does it? The Lower Zone, or called the Umbral in Portuguese, is comprised of many areas. Not just a strange dark dimension that exists parallel to our own, but also right here, on the surface of the earth.

In the book, *Memoirs of a Suicide*, by Yvonne A. Pereira, the main protagonist of the book, Camilo Castelo Branco, who committed suicide when he was going blind because of syphilis, describes what it was like awaking in the graveyard where he was buried.

"Sobbing uncontrollably, I bent over the grave that held my wretched remains. Contorting myself in terrifying convulsions of pain and rage, wallowing in a crisis of diabolical fury, I understood that I had committed suicide, that I was in the grave, but that, nevertheless, I continued to live and suffer even more, so much more than before, superlatively, abysmally so much more than before my cowardly and thoughtless act!"[20]

Hence, Camilo, while his body, six feet underground, was deteriorating, felt he was alive, with all of the loneliness, pain and suffering it entails. Walking on the face of the earth, while incarnate visitors to familial graves passed through him, oblivious to his sufferings.

Camilo then left the cemetery, trying to ascertain what was this world that he had died into?

"I continued to roam around aimlessly, feeling my way along the streets, unacknowledged by friends and admirers, a poor blind man humiliated in the afterlife thanks to the dishonor of having committed suicide; a beggar in the spirit world, famished in the darkness; a tortured, wandering ghost without a home, without shelter in the immense and infinite world of spirits; exposed to deplorable dangers; hounded by malefic entities, criminals of the spirit world, who love to use hateful traps to capture individuals going through tormenting situations like mine in order to enslave then and increase the obsessing hordes that destroy earth's societies and ruin men and women, submitting them to the vilest temptations with their deadly influence."[21]

The Lower Zone is all around us, teeming with life, not of the benevolent kind. In the book, *Nosso Lar*, psychographed by Chico Xavier and inspired by Andre Luiz; Andre, after being rescued from the Umbral by the kind spirits of the heavenly city, Nosso Lar, asks why must there be a place like the Lower Zone. He receives an answer from his friend Lisias:

> "Imagine that when we reincarnate, each of us is wearing a dirty garment that must be washed in the waters of human life. This dirty garment is our casual body, woven by our own hands during our past lives. As we share in the blessings of a new earthly opportunity once more, we usually forget our essential purpose, and instead of purifying ourselves through the effort of the cleansing process, we become even more soiled by going deeper into debt and thus imprisoning ourselves in genuine slavery. Now if we return to the world seeking a way to rid ourselves of our impurities because they are out of harmony with a higher plane, how can we expect to enter the sphere of light in an even worse state than before? Therefore, the Umbral is a region intended for the flushing away of negative mental residues. It is a sort of purgatorial zone, where one gradually burns off the refuse of the bulk of illusions acquired after having degraded the sublime opportunity of an earthly life."[22]

Lisias explains to Andre, that the Umbral begins at the crust of the earth and continues higher until it reaches the boundaries of the celestial cities. A large area that contains all those who couldn't successfully complete their mission, souls that retained their passions for material goods, hatred of their enemies, and a host of other obsessions that we are all better without.

Lisias emphasizes this point by describing the criticality of the zone.

> "The Umbral is a region of profound importance for those still on earth, for it embodies everything that is useless to the more highly evolved life. Consider how wisely Divine Providence has acted in allowing the creation of such a zone around the planet. There are legions of irresolute and ignorant souls, who are not wicked enough to be relegated to the colonies of the most dolorous expiation, nor are they sufficiently virtuous to be

admitted to the higher planes. They represent the ranks of the inhabitants in the Umbral, and they are close companions of incarnate human beings, separated from them only by vibratory laws."[23]

The phrase, "embodies everything that is useless", is the key. Useless are material goods. Useless are the passions we retain, the revenge we are plotting even up to our untimely death. Useless is our quest for a lavish lifestyle that compromised our ideals and forced us to ignore our conscience in order to gain a moment of wealth. Wealth, that is no longer with us while we reside in the Umbral.

Again, as in the Abyss, a spirit only resides in the Umbral until a personal decision to seek the way of the light is sincerely made.

## Heavenly or Celestial Cities

The quest to learn what is heaven like, starts with Allan Kardec's *The Spirits Book*. The idea of heaven is not a major preoccupation of the Spirits. They take it matter-of-fact, as a place where they still work and learn and hope to improve themselves.

Although, even the lowest rung of heaven is much superior to our planet. And yes, there are many levels, how many is not known to us. Therefore, we will concentrate on just the first level. Let's start at that question at the end of the book:

1016. In what sense is the word heaven to be understood?

"Do you suppose it to be a place like the Elysian Fields of the ancients, where all good spirits are crowded together pell-mell, with no other care than that of enjoying, throughout eternity, a passive felicity? No; it is universal space; it is the planets, the stars, and all the worlds of high degree, in which spirits are in the enjoyment of all their faculties, without having the tribulations of material life, or the sufferings inherent in the state of inferiority."[24]

Not the Elysian Fields, not the place where you leisurely waste away your days until infinity.

Another book psychographed by Francisco C. Xavier, is *Nosso Lar*, which means our home. The book was dictated by the spirit Andre Luiz, who was a doctor in Rio de Janeiro, probably in the early 1900's. This was his first book, written in 1944. The story of Nosso Lar is the journey of Andre from his death to his arrival at the celestial city of Nosso Lar. He describes his first impression upon being outside of the shelter he was taken to during his recovery;

"The spectacle of the streets impressed me. Wide avenues bordered with trees. Pure air – an atmosphere of profound spiritual tranquility. However, there was no sign of inactivity or idleness, for the city streets were crowded. Countless individuals were coming and going. Some seemed to be thinking of far-off places, but others looked at me warmly."[25]

In all descriptions we have read so far, there exists a sense of organization. Structures representing our organizations, such as well-planned roads, houses, people going about in a logical manner.

Heaven is a beautiful place to live, as Andre Luiz describes the countryside:

"The scenery in front of me was of sublime beauty. The forest was in full bloom and the fresh air was embalmed with an intoxication fragrance. It was all an extraordinary gift of color and mellow light. A large river wound its way leisurely between luxuriant grassy banks sprinkled with blue flowers. The water ran by so peacefully, so crystalline that it seemed tinted in sky blue, mirroring the color of the firmament. Wide pathways cut through the green landscape. Leafy trees were planted at regular intervals along them, offering friendly shade like pleasant shelters in the light of the comforting sun. Fancifully-shaped benches invited one to rest."[26]

The description of the vividness of the colors and the natural beauty parallels other descriptions of heaven by people who have had near death experiences.

Just as there are many areas to the Abyss and the Lower Zone, there are many different celestial cites. Each one has its own distinct character and people who speak the same language usually group together in various heavenly cities.

In the higher levels of heaven, the differences in languages are not important, since communication is via direct thought.

The glimpses of the spirit world have been presented to us so we may decide for ourselves how we shall comport ourselves on earth. We have freewill to choose our ultimate path.

# Chapter 7 – Earth – Past / Present / Future

Earth has a destiny and we are part of it. Our planet is destined to travel through distinct phases. As spirits ascend so to shall the fate of the earth.

In the book, *The Gospel According to Spiritism*, by Allan Kardec, in Chapter 3, there is an explanation of the different worlds that spirits will inhabit during their long trek toward purification.

1. Primitive World - Intended for the first incarnations of the human soul. The beings that inhabit them are, to a certain extent, rudimentary. They have the human form but are devoid of any beauty. Their instincts are not tempered by any sentiment of refinement or benevolence, or by any notions of right or wrong. Brute force is the only law. With no industry or inventions, they spend life in conquest of food. The earth was once a primitive world.

2. World of Trial and Expiation - You are living on this world. There is more evil present than good. Now you know why life is not easy, because it is not supposed to be while you are reincarnated on the planet Earth.

3. Regenerative World - Where souls still have something to expiate (pay off the debt of a past sin) and may absorb new strength by resting from the fatigue of struggle. There is still evil, but much reduced, the good outweighs the evil, consequently there is no motive for hatred or discord.

4. Happy Worlds - Where good outweighs evil. On Happy Worlds, we still retain our human form, although the senses are more acute.

5. Heavenly or Divine Worlds - Where good reigns completely, all inhabitants are purified spirits. There is no evil.

Therefore, as more spirits who incarnate on earth at a higher level, the planet shall become a regenerative world. This is the outcome we are all striving to attain.

Each of us has a part to play in this effort. Not only do we need to individually improve, but we should help our brothers and sisters whenever and wherever we are able, so collectively we can make this world a better place.

# Chapter 8 – The Reason for Reincarnation

What are the chances that we would be perfect in only one life? I know mine are non-existent. The spirit world realizes we are imperfect vessels and fragile. Hence, there is no debate in the spirit world that we need to travel through multiple lives to improve.

The central question is: how do we become pure? The answer lies within *The Spirits Book*:

*166. How can the soul that has not attained perfection during the corporeal life complete the work of purification?*

"By undergoing the trial of a new existence"

*How does the soul accomplish this new existence? Is it through it transformation as a spirit?*

"The soul, in purifying itself, undoubtedly undergoes a transformation; but, in order to effect this transformation, it needs the trial of corporeal life"

*The soul has then, many corporeal existences?*

"Yes; we all have many such existences. Those who maintain the contrary wish to keep you in the same ignorance in which they are themselves."

*It would seem to results from this statement that the soul, after having quitted one body, takes another one; in other words, that it reincarnates itself in a new body. Is it thus that this statement is to be understood?*

"Evidently so."[27]

Therefore, to ascend we must accept the task of being reborn in a physical body. There are lessons that only can be learned through a bodily existence. But why do we need to reincarnate multiple times?

## The Need for Multiple Lives

Multiple lives are required, because one life alone doesn't supply all the lessons needed for us to ascend. The spirit Andre Luiz, wrote many books, psychographed by Francisco C. Xavier, in which he goes into great depth about various aspects of the spirit realm.

In one book, he explores the need for us to be reborn over and over again. Andre Luiz was assigned to a group of spirits who assisted people leaving their earthly life in the book, *Workers of the Life Eternal*, where he witnessed numerous experiences at people's bedsides and saw firsthand the dramas that swirled around them. He weighed the frequent scenes and stories of people struggling to depart and comes to the conclusion:

> "Studying cases of death had enriched my knowledge in the field of mental science. The spirit, (eternal in essence) makes use of matter (transitory in its associations) as didactic material that evolves more and more in the spirit's never ending course of experience toward integration within the Supreme Divinity."[28]

What does Andre mean by didactic material in this instance? One of the definitions of didactic is "Teaching or intended to teach a moral lesson."[29] Therefore as we continue learning in the spirit world and travel through various physical trials on earth we accumulate moral lessons that in turn influence our physical bodies and the structure of our brain, as we are reborn. Not only is our intellectual being as spirits important, but the physical makeup of our human form is vital for our involvement on our planet and for our eventual elevation as spirits.

Given all that he had seen, Andre fully realizes the need for our multiple attempts at learning in our corporeal bodies, "Hence the reasons for the complex activities of the evolutionary road, the countless diversities, the multiplicity of social positions, the degrees of abilities and the levels of intelligence on the various planes of life."[30]

What a wonderful revelation! We all go through periods of

high social positions, living life with riches, and being the smartest person in the room. Although, we also live in the opposite positions. Truly, this knowledge must cause us all to be humble.

Being trapped in a material body affords us the opportunity to learn what is not possible to apprehend in the spirit world. While certainly, one can gather intellectual knowledge, the building of our emotions, of faith, charity, honor and love are rooted in the pain and suffering we are exposed to in the physical world. *The Spirits Book* backs up this thesis, in the secondary question to question 175:

*Would it not be happier to remain as a spirit?*

"No, no! For we should remain stationary; and we want to advance towards God."[31]

For those who believe we only need one physical life to be pure, it is as if we wanted to be the President of a large company without ever working any other job. Of course we must start in the mail room and work our way up in various positions to fully comprehend how things get done and how to survive within the culture of the organization.

No matter how pious we could have started out as a new spirit, we would still need the required know-how to gain our elevation. Only through rigorous trials do we have the right mixture of beliefs and knowledge to reincarnate with good prospects of success and to be a valued worker in the Spirit realm.

### Multiple Lives – Where?

We do need to accumulate a mountain of instances and encounters from all social, cultural, and physical environments. We are on task to build a strong foundation, upon which we can amass ever more knowledge and possess the wisdom to utilize it appropriately. So where do we begin to lay the base for our future? The answer, once again, lies in *The Spirits Book*:

*172. Do we accomplish all our different corporeal existences upon this earth?*

"Not all of them, for those existences take place in many different worlds. The world in which you now are is neither the first nor the last of these, but is one of those that are the most material, and the furthest removed from perfection."

*173. Does the soul, at each new corporeal existence pass from one world to another or can it accomplish several existences on the same globe?*

"It may live many times on the same globe, if it be not sufficiently advanced to pass into a higher one."

*We may, then, re-appear several times upon the earth?*

"Certainly."

*Can we come back to it after having lived in other worlds?"*

"Assuredly you can; you may already have lived elsewhere as upon the earth."[32]

The answers imply that we live on whatever worlds may be necessary, in order to gather the required curriculum. We are all interstellar travelers, but alas, our memories of our journeys are hidden from most of us. We regain those thoughts and remembrances when we return to the spirit world and are determined qualified to handle our memories.

# Chapter 9 – Predestination and Freewill

So why is Spiritism important to us? Out of the numerous doctrines and religions; why is this special? Because it explains the entire reason for our life.

Not just that we are here on earth to perform good deeds, to be true and honest individuals. There are many good pathways for this particular truth. What we are given is the "why" for each one of us. The answer, for each person alive on earth and in spirit around the earth, is different.

Not different in our common goal of becoming better in the drive to attain the position of a pure spirit, but in the focus given to our individual plight and our relationship with the spirit world.

Different in the meaning and sequence of daily events, why we were born of certain parents, why we have the friends that we do, why we have the job that we either love or were stuck with, every detail has a reason. The quest for these answers is why Spiritism is vitally relevant to you.

One of the most significant set of inquiries concerns the matter of your personal destiny. The discussion of the plan for your life on earth is scattered throughout Kardec's books and in psychographed books by mediums, such as Francisco C. Xavier.

In Allan Kardec's *The Gospel According to Spiritism*, the starting point for understanding your trials is in this paragraph:

"Christ said, 'Blessed are the afflicted, for they shall be comforted'.

But how can we bless suffering if we don't know why we suffer? Spiritism shows that the cause lies in previous existences and in the destiny of earth, where humans expiate their past. It shows them the purpose of their suffering as being salutary which lead to healing and which are the purification that ensures happiness in future existences. Humans understand that they deserve to suffer and they find suffering to be just. They know that this suffering aids their progress and they accept it without complaining, just as workers accept the work that will ensure their wages."[33]

Why is it important to understand our place in our destiny? According to the quote above, we should gladly accept whatever is thrown at us with a smile and work our butts off to get through it. Well, except for the few of us that possess that perfect attitude of accepting all of life's vicissitudes, we need to first comprehend what is occurring so we can meditate on it and try to mold our attitude so we may survive the ordeal the best that we can.

Are we locked and loaded into a roller coaster ride and can't get off until we expire? No, we do have freewill. To a certain extent.

For most of us, the majority of events in our life is pre-planned. As if the earth was a college and God determined exactly what courses we needed in order to improve.

This is the part that we all dread. We must acquire the experiences allotted to us to insure that we never repeat what we have done wrong in the past. You will pay for your transgressions in past lives; there is no escaping that fact. So here is the difficult and complex portion of your life; how do you combine the expiation of your wrongs with making free-will choices and doing what you desire in your life?

In the book, *Missionaries of Light*, psychographed by Francisco C. Xavier, where Andre Luiz (the spirit author of the book) is discussing the imminent birth of a spirit (Segismundo), who will undergo trials for his past wrongs. Andre asks about the plan for the spirit's life, Alexandre, Andre's teacher at the moment, replies, "Notice that I said benefit and not destiny. Many people confuse a constructive plan with fatalism. Both Segismundo and our brother Herculano have the information we are talking about, because nobody enters a school for a more or less long period without a specific purpose and without knowing the rules that he or she should obey".[34]

We are all assigned a curriculum, a course of study in the college campus that suits our needs for our present life. A learning institution that is intended to move us to a higher level. A higher level only if we are able to accumulate enough credits, or we may be required to repeat.

Andre probes deeper into the contours of the plan for Segismundo. Andre wishes to know how the trials are matched up with the past sins in Segismundo's future life and receives further information from Alexandre:

"For that reason the diagram of useful trials is drawn up beforehand, much like a student's work book at a regular school. In view of this, the diagram corresponding to Segismundo has been duly drawn up, taking in consideration the physiological cooperation of his parents, the domestic backdrop and the fraternal assistance that will be given to him by countless friends from this side. So, imagine our friend returning to a school – earth – and in doing so fulfilling a purpose; to acquire new qualities. In order to do this, he will have to submit to the rules of the school, renouncing up to a point the great freedom he used to enjoy in our environment."[35]

Hearing this, Andre is confused, he believes Alexandre's description implies a fixed destiny, since a detailed plan is formulated and all external events seemingly factored into the plan. Alexandre corrects him:

"Don't fall into the error assumed by many people. That would imply an obligatory form of spiritual conduct. Of course, individuals are reborn with a relative independence and are sometimes subjected to certain harsher conditions for educational purposes, but such imperative never suppresses the free impulse of the soul in its aim toward advancement, stagnation or fall into lower conditions. There is a plan of spiritually edifying tasks to be fulfilled by spirits who reincarnate, where their guides set the approximate quota of eternal qualities that they are prone to acquire during their transitory existence. The spirit who is returning to the physical realm can either improve this quota and surpass its superior's predictions by means of its own intensive efforts or it can fall short and go further into debt to its neighbor, scorning the holy opportunities that had been granted it."[36]

Therefore, we should think of our life like we are at school, a school we can't possibly escape until we graduate. Graduation is death, but don't think about that right now! In that school, we have classes we like and others that we either detest or find extremely boring.

In most cases we sit and dread the possibility of being called to answer something. Like all things, the bell eventually rings and we move on to the next class. We don't have the freedom to leave the school or the classroom for the time allocated to the subject. But we do have the freedom to either raise our hand and answer correctly, with enthusiasm or slink in the back and mutter something, hoping to escape that moment of terror. Guess which one gets you the better grade?

# Chapter 10 – How the Spirit World Helps Us

The spirit world is concerned with each and every one of us. Our guardian angels take no pleasure seeing us struggle, since they have all been there before. Even though, they understand that at times we need the suffering presented to us. But within the confines of letting us survive and learn from our trials, the spirit world actively guides and helps us.

During and after birth we are looked after by the spirit world. In the book, *Missionaries of the Light*, another Andre Luiz inspired book, psychographed by Chico Xavier, a well-known Spiritist and Medium from Brazil, we are told of the constant care we receive after birth;

> "Friends, Herculano will remain at Segismundo's side for seven years in his new reincarnation, at which time the reincarnation process will have been completed. After that period, his work as a friend and guide will be eased, for he will follow our brother at a distance."[37]

The spirit Herculano, who assisted during the conception and birth of Segismundo, shall stay constantly at his side for seven years. Did you ever wonder how babies can seemly survive so many dangers in their young life? Or how when young toddlers walk, looking backwards or anywhere but in front of them, why don't they bump into more objects? Because they are influenced to avoid hazards by their spirit guardian.

As to the time period of seven years, that is explained to Andre Luiz by his mentor;

> "You are aware that the human body has its vegetative activities per se, but you may not yet know that the perispiritual body, which gives form to the cellular elements, is strongly rooted in the blood. In the fetal organization, the blood elements are a gift from the mother's body. Soon after rebirth, a period of a different assimilation of organic energies takes

43

place, where the reincarnated 'self' rehearses the consolidation of its new experiences. In this new cycle of physical life, it is only at age seven that it can begin to preside on its own over the blood formation process, which is the basic element for the equilibrium of the perispiritual body or pre-existent form. Blood, therefore, can be regarded as the divine fluid that underpins our activities on the physical plane, and through its continual flow within the physiological organism, it furnishes us with a symbol of the eternal movement of the sublime energies of the Infinite Creation."[38]

The process of reincarnation, even after birth, is complex. For our spirit body to be connected to our physical body via the perispirit is a seven year long process. Not only does the child have the full time attention of their mother and father, but the spirit world supplies an invisible sentry. Continuously protecting the young child. Life is more precious than we could ever imagine.

### How we are assisted as Adults

Not only children require support from the spirit world, we do too. Again, in the book, *Missionaries of the Light*, a young woman, with small children lost her husband and was inconsolable. To supply her closure with her dead husband, the spirit world arranged a visit with him, during her sleep, when she could leave the bounds of her body. She was able to talk to him and find out that he was safe in the spirit world.

Since, our spirits can communicate directly with other spirits during our slumber, we learn many valuable lessons and have various conversations with other spirits, spirits who could reside in the spirit world or other incarnates, who had left their body. We are unable to retain exact memories of these encounters. But we do awaken with general ideas and feelings. Just like the widow did from her sleep, when her aunt asked her if she actually believed she visited her husband in a dream the night before;

"Why not?" replied the widow without blinking, "I still have the feeling of his hands on mine, and I know that God granted me such grace so that I could find my strength again to work.

44

Today I woke up totally refreshed and happy! I can face the future with new hope! I will make an effort and I shall be victorious."

"Oh Mommy, how your words console us!" exclaimed one of the little ones with bright eyes. "How I wish I could have been with you to listen to Daddy in that wonderful dream!" [39]

When you arise in the morning from a satisfying sleep and you feel good for no apparent reason, this could be a residue from a nocturnal encounter you had. Or when you leap out of bed ready to tackle that problem which had been bothering you for days, this could be the result of you finding out the solution while talking with your friends or guides in the spirit world.

If we search for the answer it will come. The spirit world wishes to supply us with all of the tools and inspirations required to prosper while we live on earth. They fully realize the day-to-day problems we encounter, complications which hinder our ability to absorb the lessons we should learn.

Therefore, like any good teacher, who wishes their students to be successful, the spirit world gently pushes us to the correct solution. We have to listen to our conscience, that governor of our behavior, with years of experience in many lives, and perform our deeds with moral clarity.

### Favors Returned

When we perform good deeds, the resulting wave of our charity rolls back toward us. People who we have aided think caring thoughts about us, spirits who assist the ones we materially help also notice our benevolence. A good example of this is found in the book, *Action and Reaction*, a spirit, a young man who died and is now watching over his mother, asks for a favor;

"My dear Assistant, our Adelino is having financial problems ... Because he helps others so much, he has been neglecting his own needs. He is always helping my poor incarnate mother, so I would ask for your help on his behalf. Just last week, my widowed mother didn't have the means to get medical treatment for my two sick brothers, so I went to him in tears and mentally begged him to help us out. He didn't hesitate for a second. Believing he was obeying his own impulses, he visited our house and gave my poor mother the money she needed … Dear Assistant! For the love of Jesus, I beg you! Don't forsake someone who has helped us out so much!"[40]

Sacrifices on our part for others, should be seen as opportunities to spread goodwill. The more goodwill we radiate, the more it will bounce back to us, enabling us to give even more. Doing well is not a zero sum game, I give and you take, no it's a positive feedback loop, with a rising crescendo of light and joy that shall surround us.

The young man is answered by the Assistant:

"Don't worry, Adelino is in a web of fraternal affinity that he has woven for himself. A lot of friends are supplying him with the resources he needs to faithfully carry out his caring task. Circumstances of a material nature will come together in his favor as a consequence of acquired merit."[41]

As you can ascertain, the little things that happen in our life, a coincidence here, a random event there that brings us unexpected joy, or the break to find a job that we always desired, could all be in response to the charity we have spread before. We are truly cared for by the spirit world. When we exhibit good behavior, our mentors wish to reward us to continue to do so.

Before we incarnate, we realize that we have much ground to cover to become better souls. Each little victory is one step closer to achieving our level of purity.

## The Spirit World Knows our Grades

While it may seem that random conversations among spirits affect the level of assistance we receive, the truth is more revealing. Once again, our old concept of Heaven as an Elysian field of bliss and comfort, must be replaced by processes that are all too familiar to us.

Once a person dies, they do not transform into a wise benevolent saint, no they are the same as before, with more intelligence and composed of different matter, but thinking along the same lines as always. The processes of watching over us and tracking our progress is the same as if we were in school.

In one of the specialized colonies in the spirit world, Almas Irmas (Spirit Sisters), they educate spirits and help them prepare for their next reincarnation. In the book, *Sex and Destiny*, another Andre Luiz inspired tome, he is told how the students who were reborn are followed:

"All reincarnate individualities connected with Almas Irmas have files containing the entire history of what they are accomplishing during their reincarnation. These files indicate not only the balance of the credits earned but also the debts acquired. This balance can be examined at any time so as to provide them with the help they deserve, depending on the loyalty they demonstrate in keeping the obligations they undertook and according to their willingness to contribute to the general good."[42]

We can't escape the fact that we must work for what we receive. This is the mundane secret of the heaven awaiting us. Processes, such as earning your living, don't disappear with death, they are just altered. Not to say, they aren't changed for the spectacularly better, where we work in our desired vocation, not just to survive. Nevertheless, we can't escape the concept of debit and credit.

To receive you must give, for as Jesus said it is always better to give than to receive, he knew what he was talking about. This wasn't just some remote ideal to make us better souls. It was practical advice on how to be successful in the spirit world.

## End of Life Assistance

For those of us that have accumulated a bounty of love along the path of our life, the spirit world lends us and our family a hand in our final passage. In the book, *Workers of the Life Eternal*, Andre Luiz is a member of a team that assist people to leave their physical bodies to return to life in the spirit world. The discarnated father of the old man dying with his family around him asks the other spirits to work with him to make his son's, Fabio, last hours pleasant. He asks the team:

"I know that Fabio's liberation will require a great deal of effort. However, I would like to help him with the last home worship in which he will physically participate at his family's side. As a general rule, a dying person's last words are more affectionately recorded in the memory of those who remain behind. For that reason, I would really like to help him say a few words of advice and encouragement to his wife."[43]

The team of spirits applied length-wise passes over Fabio's whole body, giving him the strength to participate at his last family gathering. Fabio tells his wife that he will always love her and that she should find comfort with another if that is her wish. He tells her that he will help her all he can while in the spirit realm.

Fabio's father put his hand on Fabio's forehead and inspires Fabio to say:

"I'm happy to have this opportunity to exchange ideas with you alone according to the faith we share. Significant is the absence of our old friends, who, for so many years, have accompanied us in our family prayers. There is a reason for that. We must talk about our needs, full of courage but never forgetting about the upcoming farewell. These words of the Apostle to the Gentiles are symbolic for our current situation. Just as there are mortal bodies, there are also spiritual bodies. And we can't ignore the fact that my mortal body will soon be returned to the welcoming earth, the common mother of the perishable forms in which we move about on the face of the globe. Something deep down tells me that this will perhaps be the last night that I will meet with you in this material body … At times when sleep blesses me, I feel that I am on the verge of the great deliverance … I can see that enlightened friends have been preparing my soul, and I am sure I will leave at the first opportunity. I believe all the necessary measures have already been taken to ensure our tranquility during these moments before the separation. In fact, I'm not leaving you any money but I find comfort in knowing that we have built the spiritual home of our sublime union, and it will be an indelible source of reference for our everlasting happiness …"[44]

Fabio dies peacefully later that night, while his loving family is consoled and deeply touched by his last words. What better ending to a physical life than what Fabio and his spirit helpers were able to construct. He gave spiritual advice, joy, and hope in his final moments. There would be no need to second guessing from his family about the end. No regrets of not saying the final farewell.

For the last words are not about saying goodbye forever, but a message of see you soon. For at some point of time in the future, all shall be reunited in the real world, the domain of the spirits. The universe where we actually live the vast majority of the time, for as we gain purity, we reincarnate less and less. Until, we come to the junction where to reincarnate is a choice, a mission gladly undertaken to help others as others have supported us before.

# Chapter 11 – How You Can Ascend in the Spirit Hierarchy

Since earth is a regenerative world, we must expect trials to repay our past wrongs. How should you handle these difficult lessons? Periods of life where nothing seemingly works and there are no ladders to escape?

Alexandre, Andre Luiz's mentor, from the book *Missionaries of the Light*, gives the answer, "Every plan that is drawn up in the higher spheres has the good and ascension as its basic objectives, and every soul that reincarnates, even one that finds itself in apparent desperate conditions, has resources to continue to improve."[45] Therefore, first feel certain that you do have the means to successively climb out of whatever problem you are in.

There are two important actions you can accomplish, in any situation, one is to remember the golden rule, the basis of Spiritism, "Do unto others as you would have them do unto you"; in fact go further and actively help others if at all possible. The second is to maintain a positive attitude.

In the book, *Action and Reaction*, again inspired by the spirit Andre Luiz, psychographed by Francisco C. Xavier, Andre wishes to know how an utterly bad spirit has any chance to improve themselves while they are in a difficult trial on earth. He receives this answer:

"Let's imagine a monstrous criminal who has been segregated in a prison. Accused of many crimes, he has been deprived of any of the freedom he would experience in an ordinary cell. Even in this condition, if he were to use his time in prison to willingly work for the well-being of the authorities and his fellow inmates, accepting with humility and respect the decisions of the law that is used to correct him – such attitude being the result of his free will to help or harm himself – in a short time this prisoner would begin to attract the sympathy of those about him, thus advancing surely toward self-regeneration".[46]

What we are being told is that the constraints of our fate is of our own making. Certain events and trials we must live through, our only freedom is our attitude and love for others during these times. The less we have to pay for past wrongs, the more freedom we gain to make choices to improve our souls.

For those in the midst of painful trials, pray for help and forgiveness, but above all else maintain a positive outlook and love and care for others. By this you will have paid your debt and exceeded the expectations of those that created your plan.

## How to Prepare for Future Trials

How do you build up the required strength to survive future trials? As in school, where there are periods between classes, there are periods between trials. These are the times to learn about Spiritism, participate in charity work and ponder on why you have gone through the occurrences of your life so far.

In the book, *Action and Reaction*, Andre learns about a man who at forty committed suicide. He learns that after years of suffering in the Spirit world, the man is reincarnated. Andre is told that as part of the man's trials he will have an "overwhelming temptation to commit suicide again at the exact age in which he forsook his responsibilities the previous time".[47]

So, think carefully when you have great events in your life. Contemplate about how you must have made the wrong decision in a previous existence and what steps you can take to improve.

Andre asks how can this unfortunate man resist the lure the second time? He learns that:

"If this man has not saved up renewing and educational resources through learning and the practice of fraternity so as to overcome the inevitable crisis, it will be very hard for him to avoid committing suicide again because, despite being reinforced from the outside, temptations have their starting point within us and they feed on what is already there".[48]

This is not a new trial, but a chance for a retest. If you have studied hard and learned to live with others as you should, you will pass the test. After you live through it, rejoice in the knowledge that you won't have to live through this type of event ever again.

Our destiny, our course of study in our school on earth, is not supposed to be tranquil, if it was you wouldn't be able to advance. Take comfort that which you believe are tough lessons are nothing compared to what truly failed spirits must experience. Pray for those who are in the middle of justly difficult lessons and learn to travel through yours with a positive outlook.

Graduation from the school of life is indeed death, which if you fully passed all of your classes could mean you are finished with earthly universities, but at least the reward for good grades in most classes is an even more fascinating life the next time and an exciting and fulfilling job in the spirit world before its back to the campus.

# Chapter 12 – What Have We Learned

We have presented to you, our dear reader, the basic precepts of Spiritism. First, in our normal state we are immortal spirits. Second, at our present stage of life as a spirit, we are relatively immature. Hence, we are carefully guided, think nursery school, watched, measured and loved.

Whatever mess we make of our life, we are loved. Expectations are low and most of us barely pass. In order to teach us to get along with all of the other spirits in the universe, we must have a minimum amount of training.

The training, suffering through successive lives in various circumstances, may seem harsh to us, but in the perspective of eternity or billions of years depending on how you like to think of it, a span of fifty to ninety years on earth for each set of courses is less than the amount of time you place a two year old in a corner after a temper tantrum.

Are you a Spiritist yet? Even though, indirectly I have called you, and me of course, immature and relatively ignorant. Isn't there a sense of momentary relief? Finally you have the answer on how in the heck could you have done so many things wrong in your life.

Thirdly, as part of our training, our lives on earth follow a script. The major events are planned, our reactions and choices within those acts are the factors on which we are graded.

We are expected to learn from our mistakes and to demonstrate our new found talent in the next life when we are shown new obstacles.

When we have wronged others, our script sends us onto a stage where in turn we get to play the part of the victim. Seeing both sides of the story provides us with the rounding we require.

The milestones of our life is not all payback. As children are sent on field trips to absorb new sights and sounds, we too are provided new circumstances for learning.

All that I have written barely scratches the surface. For example, I have an entire book on how to explore your destiny, another on the many facets of reincarnation. I have the introductions to my books at the end of this book. I have written them so you may dive deeper into the meaning of your life.

There are so many types of experiences we must have in order to fulfill our graduate requirements. Such as, one life spent in the lap of luxury, to determine whether we are able to maintain our humility and kindness towards others or like so many, become an irrational tyrant, because we can.

If what you have read interests you, I invite you to continue seeking and learning about Spiritism. Your life will benefit. You will reach a mountaintop from which you will be able to look down at your life from a position of certainty. Safe in the awareness that whatever hurdles you encounter, are merely small bumps in the road to your eventual perfection.

# Your Exploration Continues...

Learn more about Spiritism in my blog at:
http://www.nwspiritism.com.

To assist you in understanding more about Spiritism, I have written three other books.

- Explore Your Destiny – Since Your Life's Path is (mostly) Predetermined
- The Case for Reincarnation – Your Path to Perfection
- What Really Happens During Near Death Experiences According to Spiritism – 12 NDEs Explained and Explored

In the next sections are the introductions to my books.

Join us on Facebook at: https://www.facebook.com/nwspiritism

Join our discussion group on Spiritism at:
https://www.facebook.com/groups/Spiritist/

Go to the source of Spiritism and read Allan Kardec's books. The two I find most interesting are:

1. The Spirits Book

2. The Gospel According to Spiritism

Follow the life of Andre Luiz as he rises to the celestial city of Nosso Lar and he experiences different aspects of how the spirit realm loves and guides us is one of the most satisfying reads in my life. There are thirteen books in the series, only eleven in English at this time, and I urge you to read all of them in order.

1. Nosso Lar

2. The Messengers

3. Missionaries of the Light

I hope you enjoyed this very brief introduction to Spiritism.

## Explore Your Destiny – Since Your Life's Path is (mostly) Predetermined

Do you wonder if you have an important call with destiny? That you have been selected for something? A cause of a higher purpose?

Well you have been chosen and the why, when, where and how is the subject of this book.

Your life isn't one of just survival through the daily grind of life. The ups and downs of what you have been through are all for a purpose. Every key experience you have had, every calamity that befell you and each relationship that went south or well are part of your overall story. Each major event in your life has been planned.

Have you felt this could be true? Was there even a hint of recognition that certain events occurred for a purpose? And that you were seemingly on a train headed for some unknown destination and you couldn't get off?

This is because within your deepest thoughts, unconsciously, you recognize that you are part of a greater plan. A plan that has been drawn up with your improvement in mind.

There is an answer to your intuition and questions. The answer is wonderful and your part in the drama you are leading is fascinating. Once you realize the total environment in which you reside in, you will recognize that your life is not dreary, but a heart stopping adventure, a roller coaster ride that drives you forward into an unimaginable future.

*Explore Your Destiny* is divided into four sections. Each section supplies one more piece of the puzzle for you to place, so you can look at your life's arc with new insights.

1.  Why – Why are we here and why must we live what we are living through right now? It's the age old expression, that we all say at one time or another, "Why me?" Well there is a reason and it will be explained to you.

2.  When – In what period along your souls timeline is all of this happening? Yes, there is a greater context of your soul, which you may not be aware of. Knowing your relative position in the path to perfection will guide you to understanding your current life.

3.  How – How does all of this occur? How does the entire process affect your destiny and actions? What are the rules of the game? Knowing the structure and comprehending the basic laws that direct your life provides you with a point of view that will put everything into perspective.

4.  Where – Where is this world that plans our destiny? Are there good places to be and are there bad? Where does the earth fit into the logical structure? You will see where the regions that you are striving to attain are and

where you may be living in your not-to-distant future.

I hope that after reading this book you will have a new view of your life. A view that allows you to look at your circumstances from afar and identify the turning points in your personal destiny. I want you to be in that high level observation tower where you can dispassionately evaluate your life and calmly proceed through the good and bad times. Always keeping your eye on the ball of what your true goal really is – Your triumph in the Spirit and Physical worlds.

My book is available at Amazon; Explore Your Destiny – Since Your Life's Path is (mostly) Predetermined.

To fully understand the emotions of the people living through their NDEs and the actions of the spirit world in sending people back to earth, a review of how and why we travel through multiple lives is helpful.

You have lived multiple lives. At times you have been rich, poor, a servant and a slave. Maybe even a King or a Queen, at the least a member of the minor nobility.

Many famous people in the past have believed in reincarnation, such as Thomas Edison and Sir Arthur Conan Doyle. They both believed in the spirit world and made attempts to communicate with the world beyond.

There is a realm, a universe greater than ours and it is filled with intelligences that we can only wonder at. There are spirits around the earth who are actively helping and guiding us in our planning and during our actual incarnations.

You are interested in this book and in the topic because you know, in your heart that we are not merely chemical elements that dissolve with death. There must be something more, you know this, because of your own intuition, experiences and beliefs.

There are too many unexplained phenomena for there to be nothing after death. How do some people have past life memories? Why do children remember past lives and then lose the ability after a certain age? How can some people know the future? And more importantly, why do you have premonitions that come true? How could you know what could happen with such certainty?

Reincarnation is a tenet in many religions, such as Hinduism and Buddhism, and is frequently mentioned as parts of varied sects of Christianity and Judaism. It is the concept whereby we have a spirit, in which we retain our central personalities and memories, while in the spirit world, but lose our memories while in a physical form.

This book is here to answer your questions;

1. Why do we reincarnate?

2. How does the process work?

3. How many reincarnations must we have?

4. What memories do we retain from our previous lives?

5. Do we have control over our reincarnations?

6. Why must we suffer?

7. How may I insure my next life is better?

8. How may I progress to being a perfected spirit?

These questions are answered through the Doctrine of Spiritism. When, in the 1850's, the spirit world determine it was time for the human race to assimilate this knowledge in the hopes it would led us to understand the need to improve our spirituality and to achieve a better balance between our desire for material goods versus our desire to be a better person.

Explore what is your role and where you are in this journey. Determine your place and your future. Find out the reasons for your current tribulations and how to, not only survive your trials, but prosper through them.

Your journey in different bodies at different times in different circumstances is not without a purpose. You began as a primitive soul and through successive lives; you are being molded into a perfect spirit.

Dive deeper into all facets of reincarnation; my book is available at Amazon; The Case for Reincarnation – Your Path to Perfection

# What Really Happens During Near Death Experiences, According to Spiritism

### 12 NDE's Explained and Explored

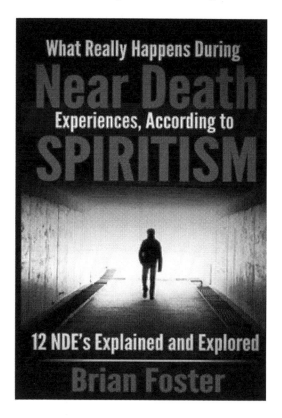

Why are we interested in Near Death Experiences (NDE)? With the advent of the internet, social media allows masses of people to more efficiently pool together shared experiences than at any other time in history. What was once an isolated phenomenon is now a common occurrence. Whereas, in times past a simple farmer or a rich landowner who would be able to pull back from death, their story, if they chose to tell it, would be a solitary happenstance. Easily explained away or believed. It made no difference, since the significance of the account would be eventually dismissed as an outlying data point.

The recent improvement in the speed and efficiency of human

communication in conjunction with modern medical methods of assisting the human body to recover after trauma has supported the explosion of accounts. And as the interpretations of each individual who returned became widely known and disseminated, others choose to finally reveal their own personal story.

Therefore a small bookshelf of NDEs is now becoming a library. Recollections from every country, culture, language and age group now reside in the great internet cloud. A mountain of data, which can no longer be wished away or ignored. The parallels and common themes from all corners of the world preclude everyone's account to be merely mass hysteria. NDEs aren't in the territory of alien encounters. Doctors, lawyers, professors, engineers, sales and service people are reporting in. Telling us similar refrains, with the added mystery of some NDEs where the person either saw or is told of events that they could not have possibly known in their current state. Taken as a whole, the only conclusion is that something must be happening, beyond our comprehension.

What Really Happens During Near Death Experiences – 12 NDEs Explained and Explored is available at Amazon.

# __Author__

Stay in touch with the author via:

Spiritist Blog: http://www.nwspiritism.com

Facebook: https://www.facebook.com/nwspiritism

Facebook group to discuss Spiritism: (please request to join)
https://www.facebook.com/groups/Spiritist/

Twitter: https://twitter.com/intent/user?screen_name=nwspiritism

If you liked *Spiritism 101 – The Third Revelation*, please post a review at Amazon.

# Copyright

# Bibliography

Denis, L. (2012). *Life and Destiny.* Forgotten Books.

Kardec, A. (2006). *Heaven and Hell.* Brasilia (DF), Brasil: International Spiritist Council.

Kardec, A. (2008). *The Gospel According to Spiritism.* Brasilia (DF): International Spiritist Council.

Kardec, A. (2009). *Genesis - Miracles and Predictions according to Spiritism.* Brasilia (DF), Brasil: International Spiritist Council.

Kardec, A. (2010). *The Spirits Book.* Guildford, UK: White Crow Books.

Swedenborg, E. (1758). *Heaven and Hell.* Europe: A Publice Domain Book.

Wikipedia. (2014, August 21). *Camilo Castelo Branco.* Retrieved from Wikipedia: http://en.wikipedia.org/wiki/Camilo_Castelo_Branco

Xavier, F. C. (2004). *In the Domain of Mediumship.* New York: Spiritist Alliance of Books, Inc.

Xavier, F. C. (2008). *The Messengers.* Philadelphia, PA: Allan Kardec Educational Society.

Xavier, F. C. (2008). *Workers of the Life Eternal.* Brasilia (DF) - Brazil: International Spiritist Council.

Xavier, F. C. (2009). *And Life Goes On.* Brasilia (DF), Brasil: International Spiritist Council.

Xavier, F. C. (2009). *In the Greater World.* Brasilia (DF), Brazil: International Spiritist Council.

Xavier, F. C. (2009). *Missionaries of the Light.* Brasilia (DF), Brazil: International Spiritist Council.

Xavier, F. C. (2010). *Action and Reaction.* Brasilia (DF), Brazil: International Spiritist Council.

Xavier, F. C. (2010). *Nosso Lar.* Brasilia - (DF), Brazil: International Spiritist Council.

Xavier, F. C. (2011). *Between Heaven and Earth.* Brasilia (DF), Brazil: International Spiritist Council.

Xavier, F. C. (2011). *In the Realms of Mediumship.* Brasilia (DF), Brazil: EDICEI.

Xavier, F. C. (2011). *On the Way to the Light.* Brasilia (DF), Brazil: International Spiritist Council.

Xavier, F. C. (2013). *Liberation.* Brasilia (DF), Brazil: International Spiritist Council.

Xavier, F. C. (2013). *Sex and Destiny.* Miami, FL: EDICEI of America.

[1] Wikipedia, "Allan Kardec", n.d., http://en.wikipedia.org/wiki/Allan_Kardec, (accessed May 10, 2014)

[2] Wikipedia, "Allan Kardec", n.d., http://en.wikipedia.org/wiki/Allan_Kardec, (accessed May 10, 2014)

[3] Spirit Writings, "Allan Kardec Biography:, n.d., http://www.spiritwritings.com/kardec.html (accessed May 10, 2014)

[4] KARDEC, Allan. The Gospel According to Spiritism, EDICEI , pp. 129-131

[5] KARDEC, Allan, The Spirits Book, White Crow Books, Ques. 1, p.60

[6] KARDEC, Allan, The Spirits Book, White Crow Books, p.64

[7] KARDEC, Allan, The Spirits Book, White Crow Books, Ques. 10, p.63

[8] KARDEC, Allan, The Spirits Book, White Crow Books, Ques. 11, p.63

[9] KARDEC, Allan, The Spirits Book, White Crow Books, Ques. 81, p.97

[10] KARDEC, Allan, The Spirits Book, White Crow Books, Ques. 88, p.99

[11] KARDEC, Allan, The Spirits Book, White Crow Books, Ques. 87, p.99

[12] KARDEC, Allan, Genesis, EDICEI, pp. 123-124

[13] KARDEC, Allan, Genesis, EDICEI, p. 124

[14] XAVIER, Francisco C. On the Way to the Light, EDICEI, pp. 19-20

[15] XAVIER, Francisco C. On the Way to the Light, EDICEI, pp. 25-26

[16] Xavier, F.C. Liberation, EDICEI, pp. 53-54

[17] Xavier, F.C. Liberation, EDICEI, p. 54

[18] Xavier, Francisco C. Between Heaven and Earth, EDICEI,

pp.137-138

[19] Xavier, F.C. Nosso Lar, EDICEI, p. 17

[20] Pereira, Y. A. Memoirs of a Suicide, EDICEI, p. 46

[21]Pereira, Y. A. Memoirs of a Suicide, EDICEI, p. 47

[22] Xavier, F.C. Nosso Lar, EDICEI, pp. 74-75

[23] Xavier, F.C. Nosso Lar, EDICEI, p. 75

[24] KARDEC, Allan. The Spirits Book, White Crow Books, Question 1016, p xxx

[25] Xavier, F.C. Nosso Lar, EDICEI, p 53

[26] Xavier, F.C. Nosso Lar, EDICEI, p 64

[27] Kardec, A., The Spirits Book, Guildford, UK, White Crow Books, Chap. 4, ques. 166, p. 141

[28] XAVIER, Francisco C. Workers of the Lifer Eternal, Brasilia (DF),EDICEI, p. 365

[29] dictionary.reference.com/browse/didactic

[30] XAVIER, Francisco C. Workers of the Lifer Eternal, Brasilia (DF), EDICEI, p. 365

[31] Kardec, A., The Spirits Book, Guildford, UK, White Crow Books, Chap. 4, ques. 175, p. 144

[32] Kardec, A., The Spirits Book, Guildford, UK, White Crow Books, Chap. 4, ques. 172-173, pp. 143-144

[33] KARDEC, Allan. The Gospel According to Spiritism, EDICEI Cap. 5, item 4

[34] XAVIER, Francisco C. Missionaries of the Light, EDICEI, p. 225

[35] XAVIER, Francisco C. Missionaries of the Light, EDICEI p. 225

[36] XAVIER, Francisco C. Missionaries of the Light, EDICEI p. 226

[37] Xavier, F.C. Missionaries of the Light, EDICEI, pp. 217-218

[38] Xavier, F.C. Missionaries of the Light, EDICEI, pp. 219-220

[39] Xavier, F.C. Missionaries of the Light, EDICEI, pp. 154-155

[40] Xavier, F.C. Action and Reaction, EDICEI, pp. 210-211

[41] Xavier, F.C. Action and Reaction, EDICEI, p. 211

[42] Xavier, F.C. Sex and Destiny, EDICEI, p. 289

[43] Xavier, F.C. Sex and Destiny, EDICEI, p. 315

[44] Xavier, F.C. Sex and Destiny, EDICEI, pp. 318-319

[45] XAVIER, Francisco C. Missionaries of the Light, EDICEI p.

226

[46] XAVIER, Francisco C. Action and Reaction, EDICEI p. 88
[47] XAVIER, Francisco C. Action and Reaction, EDICEI p. 89
[48] XAVIER, Francisco C. Action and Reaction, EDICEI p. 90

90596062R00042

Made in the USA
Middletown, DE
25 September 2018